OUTER SPACE

Elisa Peters

PowerKiDS
press™
New York

Published in 2013 by The Rosen Publishing Group, Inc.
29 East 21st Street, New York, NY 10010

Copyright © 2013 by The Rosen Publishing Group, Inc.

First Edition

Editor: Amelie von Zumbusch
Book Design: Kate Laczynski

Photo Credits: Cover Astrophotography by Terry Hancock used with permission/Flickr/Getty Images; pp. 4, 10 Shutterstock.com; p. 6 © Photodisc; p. 8 David Nunuk/All Canada Photos/Getty Images; p 12 Medioimages/Photodisc/Thinkstock; pp. 14, 24 (planet) Space Frontiers/Dera/Taxi/Getty Images; p. 16 Visuals Unlimited, Inc./Gustav Verderber/Visuals Unlimited/Getty Images; pp. 18, 24 (comet) Dan Schechter/Science Photo Library/Getty Images; pp. 20, 24 (meteoroid) Peter Sherrard/Taxi/Getty Images; p. 22 Alan Dyer/Flickr/Getty Images.

Library of Congress Cataloging-in-Publication Data

Peters, Elisa.
 Outer space / by Elisa Peters. — 1st ed.
   p. cm. — (Powerkids readers: the universe)
 Includes index.
 ISBN 978-1-4488-7390-6 (library binding) — ISBN 978-1-4488-7469-9 (pbk.) —
ISBN 978-1-4488-7542-9 (6-pack)
 1. Astronomy—Juvenile literature. 2. Outer space—Exploration—Juvenile literature. I. Title.
 QB46.P48 2013
 520—dc23
                    2011050054

Manufactured in the United States of America

CPSIA Compliance Information: Batch #CS12PK: For Further Information contact Rosen Publishing, New York, New York at 1-800-237-9932

CONTENTS

Outer space is huge.

6

It starts where Earth's air ends.

It has many stars.

Stars make light.

The Sun is the closest star.

14

Eight **planets** circle it.

Comets have long tails.

The tails always point away from the Sun.

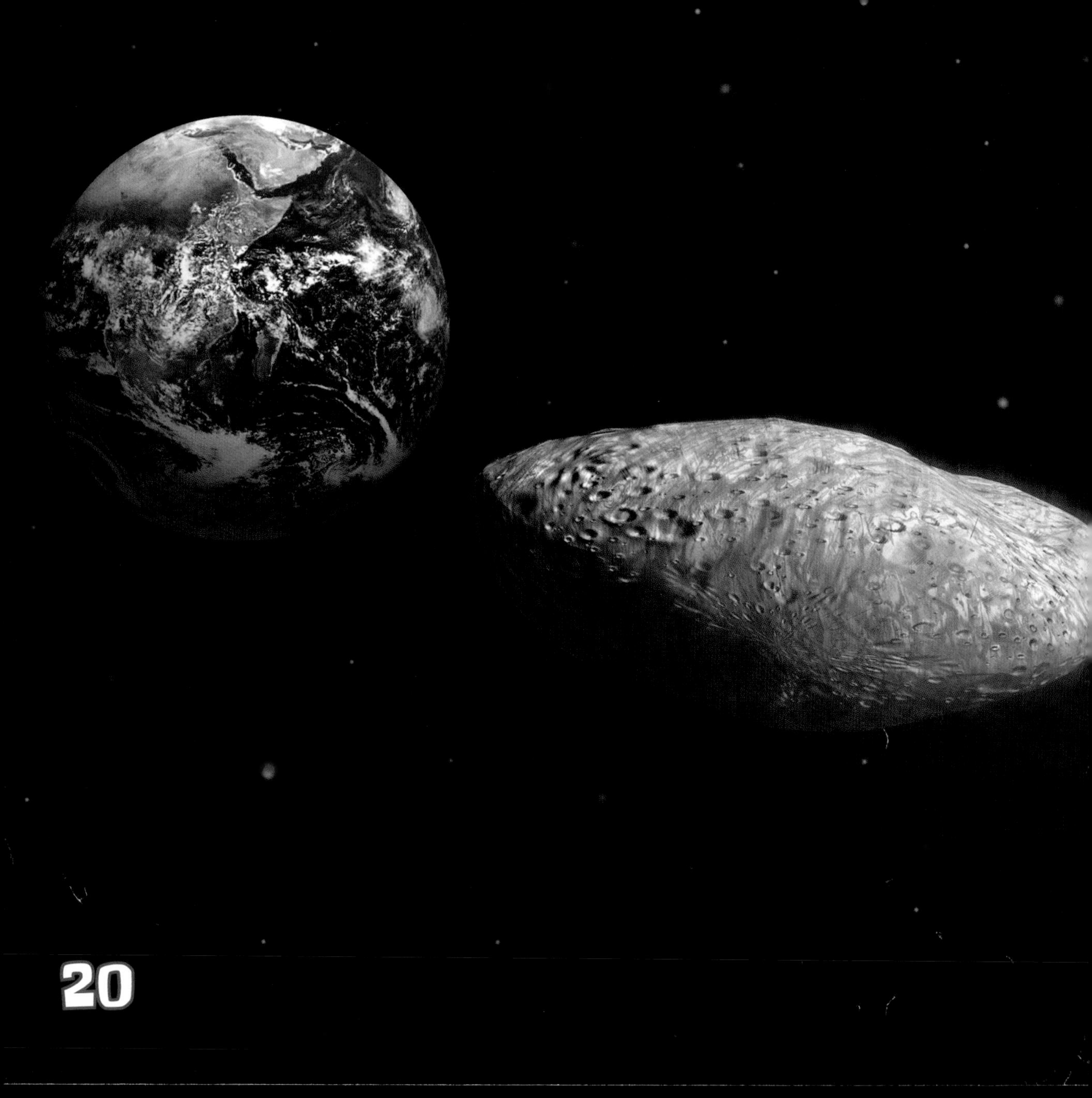

Meteoroids are bits of rock.

They burn up when they get near Earth.

WORDS TO KNOW

comet

meteoroid

planet

INDEX

WEBSITES

Due to the changing nature of Internet links, PowerKids Press has developed an online list of websites related to the subject of this book. This site is updated regularly. Please use this link to access the list:
www.powerkidslinks.com/pkrtu/space/